IRELAND

IRELAND

SINGULAR IMAGES

DONOVAN WYLIE

ANDRE DEUTSCH

First published in Great Britain in 1994 by
André Deutsch Limited
106 Great Russell Street
London WC1B 3LJ

ISBN 0 233 98899 8

Cataloguing-in-Publication data available for this title
from the British Library

Design by Jeffrey Sains
Printed in Great Britain
by Ebenezer Baylis & Son Limited, Worcester

For Patrick and Conor

INTRODUCTION

I distinguished myself at the age of ten by becoming Northern Ireland's yo-yo champion but, a competitive occupation, the pressure became too great and at twelve I gave it all up for one of relative ease – photography. I bought a camera for £10 from a school friend. It had belonged to his father who had died some years earlier. It was very old; a twin lens reflex camera. Pressing the shutter was an uncertain business: sometimes it would work, sometimes it would open and close only how and when it felt like it.

Growing up in Belfast in the seventies and early eighties I saw more of the city on television than through actually living there. Perhaps it was this which made me determined not to take pictures of the conflict, or anything to do with conflict, as that was too easy, too obvious. So while everyone else was ignoring ordinary life, that was what came to excite me. I'd seen the news too often. The idea of creating pictures I hadn't seen before was what gave me a buzz.

First, I wandered through Belfast photographing the obvious: a man looking out of a taxi window, a woman leaning against a wall. I was looking for people going about the mundane flow of their lives, wanting to focus on the *detail* of day-to-day existence, possibly as a means of seeking answers to greater questions about my own city.

In a curious way, you become very intimate with these people you have watched and heard, even become affectionate to those who you begin to understand. But all the while you never exchange a word; you remain invisible. The majority of the photographs are taken without the subjects' knowledge. On the occasions when they do glimpse you, they don't take you seriously because you are so young and, seemingly, so innocent.

A couple of years later I began travelling all around Northern Ireland. My family allowed me to do so at weekends and in the school holidays. Much of the excitement was just being out of Belfast. Then, Ballymena was as thrilling to me as, say, Canton is now. But I took very bad pictures. The towns were very quiet compared to home; there were fewer people and I tried too hard. Still, it was an exciting time.

About six months after this I spent some time with a group of gypsies at the top of the Glen Road in Belfast and did manage to catch some good images. I felt compelled to experiment with the photo-story, but I hadn't yet learnt the discipline and the patience required for it. It is necessary to be extremely focused about your theme and to have your audience clearly in mind. To keep them looking and interested, there must be some sort of narrative. It takes years to learn how to do this effectively. The problem was that gypsies were a subject in themselves. The street, on the other hand, offered infinite subjects, at speed, and I wanted, freely, to tackle them all.

Firing off photographs in my usual fashion enabled me to at least try to satisfy an overwhelming curiosity. For example, if I saw a man coming out of the dole office, cash in hand, I would wonder what he was going to do with it and there was nothing to stop me, camera in my hand, from following him. So follow him I would until the last possible moment – which was invariably when he went into a bar, which I was too young to enter.

I left school at fifteen and worked as a photographer in Santa's Grotto in order to earn good money to fund a lone trip around Ireland. The Grotto was in a department store in Protestant east Belfast. Santa tactfully recommended that I change my somewhat Catholic Christian name to a more Protestant one – Donald. Being there didn't make great pictures but it was an extraordinary insight into the workings of the poor Belfast family and an all-round unforgettable experience (I lost my virginity on Santa's sledge, to Santa's PA).

In six weeks I had saved enough money to make a short, rootless wander around Ireland. These photographs are from that time and most have never been published before. In many ways this trip launched my career because the photographs led to my first book, *32 Counties* which in turn led to the second, *The Dispossessed*. A few of these pictures are taken from those books.

I did worry about portraying Ireland wrongly. I spent hours in bookshops looking at photographic books of Ireland already published. They all seemed to be coffee-table books, glossy and tendentious, highlighting Belfast's troubles (which I sorely resented) and looking at the rest of the country through rosy-coloured lenses. I couldn't understand how people could buy such books. I aimed to make a book that was more real, straightforward, natural. I wanted to wait for things to rise to the surface as opposed to having to dig gratuitously beneath it. I even looked up farmers, bootmakers and blacksmiths in the *Yellow Pages* to ring and ask if I could photograph them, until I realised it was pointless to try to make a book in this way, so contrived. It contradicted with my idea of photographing Ireland spontaneously.

So I ended up hitching to Dublin, with no obligations to do anything I didn't want to do. I'd been to Dublin before but this was the first time I'd had the opportunity to wander about, as I used to do in Belfast. It was much more alive than Belfast, but poorer, tougher, sadder. It was like going to the other end of the world. I took a lot of photographs in the city centre, because I knew that there I'd see a greater cross-section of people. I tried to catch them in the very act of living. In an ideal world, I wished I could have just blinked my eyes.

I continued on my way, hitching throughout Ireland. There was no pressure to be at a certain place at a certain time. I stayed in grim little B & B's with greasy breakfasts or, occasionally, I'd rent a room in a family house and watch TV with them, as if I was at home with my own family. I was always welcomed.

Every day I would get up at six and just wander for hours. By three or four in the afternoon I would hitch to the next place, have a beer when I arrived, sometimes two, then find a place to stay; nights, I would walk about again. The odd time I slept rough because I had a tent but I was useless at it, always pitching it in a bog, or on a wasp's nest. Sometimes I wasn't even able to find a bog or a wasp's nest and would fall asleep on a park bench.

It is so liberating to be able to play truant with a camera as I did then, not to have a specific subject, or to be led by a particular story. It's amazing, the ambitious things you end up doing when you have that freedom. At sixteen I found myself, visually, taking on ideas that were unexpectedly profound. As you get older, it is all too easy to become too constrained by what society demands today of the professional photographer – the combined limitations of photo-journalism and the picture editor's imagination. If you are not careful you can lose what you once had.

Limerick was the roughest town but visually very

interesting. I took a lot of photographs of mothers and fathers: the mothers carrying the burden – the children and the shopping – and the fathers, in a typical way, always two steps behind. As time went on I realised I was producing this quite bleak impression of Ireland but also a beautiful one. There was effort portrayed there; a struggle, yet not failure. It was sad but not depressing because it was admirable, honest and real.

After a while I started to hate the hitching. The longer I was on the road, the more scruffy I became, so the longer I had to wait for lifts. I used to try to smarten myself up as best I could. If my shoes were dirty, I would clean them in a puddle; if there was a hole in my jeans, I would try to cover it with my jacket. There was an art to hitching. I'd stare at the driver, willing him or her to stop. It often worked.

On one occasion, in Donegal, it was getting dark and I was getting desperate for a lift. A priest drove up to me and said 'The Virgin Mary told me to stop, she said to me "Give that man a lift."' I got in the car with him. As we drove along he asked if I'd go to church with him. I could hardly say no. We went up a long driveway to this very remote, very beautiful country church. My father is Protesant, my mother is Catholic but they brought me up with no religion, so I could make up my own mind. I'd never been inside a church before. I knew as much about Catholicism as I did Janeism. And there was this priest reciting the Hail Mary, wanting me to join in and I was completely unable to. I didn't know a single word so I had to mumble, pathetically trying to pretend I did. I was really quite embarrassed.

The priest then went to Confession and afterwards urged me to do the same. I said I'd really rather not but he insisted, so I went in to keep him happy. I closed the door and started looking around me. Then I tapped on the screen. 'Where's the seat?' I asked, and was surprised to be told, 'Kneel, son, kneel.' It took me a moment to catch on. I was forced to admit to him that I was a rather lapsed Catholic. As I left the priest peeped out of his box, lifted his spectacles and gave me a look of utter bewilderment.

In Tipperary I fell in love with a girl who worked in a restaurant and lived alone. I walked her home, dying to go in and spend the night with her. But she wouldn't let me. She was a Catholic girl. I said I'd be back in a week and together we would go to Galway. I never returned so perhaps I wasn't really in love. But she was unbelievably beautiful.

The trip ended hitch-hiking from Cavan. A man picked me up, we drove for about two hours and he dropped me literally at my front door. It was strange to be home. I had spent so much time in the south of Ireland – so different from the north, so much less tense, so easy-going.

I must have taken something like two hundred reels of film during that trip. These, and other photographs I took of Ireland in passing over the next two years, are a very singular set of pictures. They laid the foundation of what I do now. I'll probably never be able to take their like again because I'll never be that age again and so startled by seeing life outside my street for the first time.

1

Storm over Belfast

Belfast

Belfast

Armagh

Belfast

Belfast

Belfast

Belfast

Belfast

Belfast

2

Belfast

Belfast

Belfast

Dublin

Belfast

Dublin

3

County Mayo

Atlantic Ocean

County Galway

County Galway

County Kerry

County Clare

4

County Tyrone

County Meath

County Tyrone

County Wicklow

County Dublin

County Kilkenny

County Waterford

County Clare

County Tyrone

County Louth

County Cork

County Leitrim

County Down

County Tipperary

County Galway

County Laois

County Meath

County Waterford

County Cork

County Fermanagh

County Wicklow

County Roscommon

County Roscommon

County Sligo